IRELAND'S RAILWAYS PAST AND PRESENT

DUBLIN

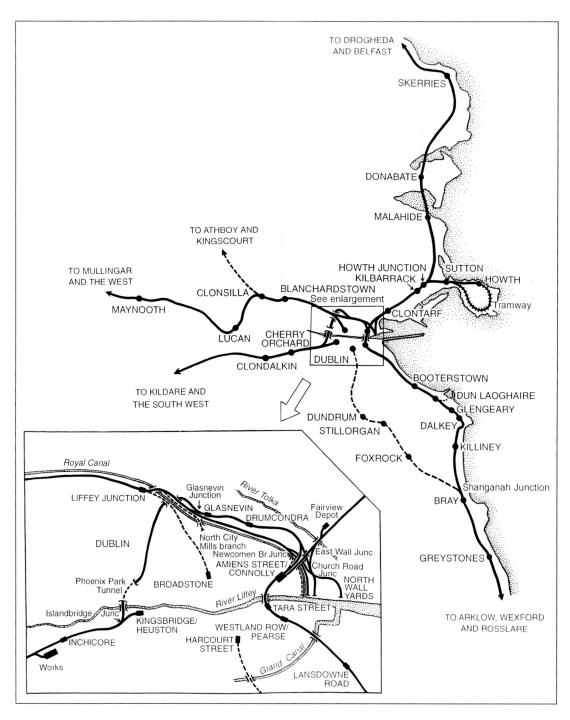

A map of the railways of the Dublin area, showing locations featured in the photographs or mentioned in the text.

IRELAND'S RAILWAYS PAST AND PRESENT

DUBLIN

MICHAEL H. C. BAKER

• A PAST & PRESENT BOOK •

from

○ *The CUMHA Collection* ○

For Sam
14.3.76 – 4.12.96

© Michael H. C. Baker 1997 and 2005

First published as *The Railways of Ireland Past and Present: Dublin* in 1997
This revised, updated and reformatted edition first published 2005

British Library Cataloguing in Publication Data

A catalogue record for this book is available from the British Library.

ISBN 1 85895 250 6
ISBN 978 1 85895 250 5

Past & Present Publishing Ltd
The Trundle
Ringstead Road
Great Addington
Kettering
Northants NN14 4BW

Tel/Fax: 01536 330588
email: sales@nostalgiacollection.com
Website: www.nostalgiacollection.com

Map drawn by Christina Siviter

Printed and bound in Great Britain

○ *The CUMHA Collection* ○
is an imprint of Past & Present Publishing Ltd

No 88, an Aspinall 'D14' ('60') Class 4-4-0 of 1886, leaves Dublin Kingsbridge with a Cork express in GSWR days.
In the summer of 1995, after many years' absence, the 'Radio Train' was reinstated, the carriages being the 'Executive' train with additional Mark IIIs. It is seen here in August 1996, a few minutes before its 08.50 departure from the now renamed Heuston station for Killarney, hauled by Class 201 Co-Co No 223 *Abhainn na hAinnire/River Anner.* *Author's collection/MHCB*

Contents

'I3' Class 0-6-2T No 670 entering Dublin's Westland Row, as Pearse station then was, with a train from Bray in June 1956.

In August 1996 a DART departs from Pearse. The cab end of a 1989 push-pull, made up of modified BR Mark III carriages, can be seen in the left foreground. *Neil Sprinks/MHCB*

Introduction

There was a time, around 40 years ago when I first visited Ireland, when the railway network in Dublin was seen primarily as the hub of the long-distance system, and its contribution to commuter travel not much more than peripheral. One suburban line, that out of Harcourt Street, had just closed, the huge fleet of modern, double-deck Leyland Titan buses made a profit and served the city well, while the number of families owning a car was small, although increasing rapidly. The city was also growing apace, with estates of grey, concrete houses spreading north, west and south. If any thought was given to how the inhabitants would travel to and from work – and not much was – the assumption was that it would be either by bus or private car; that is, unless they happened to live close to the lines that served the coastal communities from Bray to Howth.

When my father-in-law moved into his brand new house in Glasnevin in 1947 it was within walking distance of open country yet close enough to his city centre office for him to cycle home for lunch. His Vauxhall Wyvern, which was bought for weekend outings and holidays in Kerry, was the wonder of the neighbourhood. By the late 1960s Glasnevin was an inner suburb, nearly every family in the road had a car, and Dublin had the most outdated road network of any city in Western Europe. Traffic congestion was beginning to paralyse it.

The absorption of the Great Northern Railway (GNR) routes in the Republic by CIE in 1958 meant that services to the north and south of the city could be integrated. Diesel railcars, introduced in the early 1950s, operated quite a lot of these, some cascaded from main-line work. Their relatively few and rather narrow doors with high footsteps meant that they were not ideal for suburban work. Although quite a lot of the locomotive-hauled trains could boast modern carriages, these too were basically modified, or often actual down-graded main-line ones, with few doors. The only really suitable ones were some ancient Great Southern & Western Railway (GSWR) and early Great Southern Railway (GSR) wooden-bodied compartment stock, but these were overdue for the breaker's torch.

By the end of the 1960s the railcars were also coming to the end of their useful lives, but although electrification had been mooted for years, the will to fund this simply wasn't there, and Inchicore Works came up with the ingenious but essentially stop-gap solution of converting the railcars to push-pull units in charge of re-engined C Class diesels, redesignated the 201 Class. Thus things staggered on for a decade and more, both push-pull and hauled carriages becoming shabbier and more out-of-date. Despite dieselisation, steam-heating remained the norm, the doors were no wider, the seating was re-arranged to give more standing space, and investment was practically non-existent. Still the city grew, and suburban rail travel, chronically overcrowded at peak periods, was not a pleasant experience.

Although there had been attempts long ago to introduce a suburban service on the lines to the west, the termini at Kingsbridge and Broadstone were both so far from the city centre that they had, not surprisingly, failed. However, in 1981 the first suburban service for many decades other than along the coast began when push-pull units began to operate between Connolly (the former Amiens Street) and Maynooth, 16 miles distant on the former Midland Great Western Railway (MGWR) main line to Mullingar and the west, stopping at stations long derelict but now rebuilt.

This was the beginning of the revival of suburban rail travel in the Dublin area, which continues to this day and which features on many of the pages of this book. The biggest advance of all was the inauguration on 23 July 1984 of the ingeniously named DART, the Dublin Area Rapid Transit. Helped by funding from the EEC, this electrified system running from Bray to Howth has utterly transformed the attitude of Dubliners to railway travel.

Over the years many old stations have been re-opened and new ones built, while extensions have been added, south and north, to Greystones and Malahide. On 16 May 1994 the first ever suburban service out of Heuston began with newly introduced Japanese-built 'Arrow' diesel railcars, operating the 50-minute run to and from Kildare, with something over 30 trains in each direction calling at re-opened or new intermediate stations. Railcars once dominated both suburban and long-distance travel, in the 1950s and '60s, and now they are back, Iarnrod Eireann (Irish Rail) owning 144 by the end of 2004 with more due to enter service. They mostly serve the commuter routes north, south and west from Dublin.

The transformation in Ireland, and in Dublin in particular, from a relatively poor country, at least by Western European standards, to one of the world's richest, has been extraordinary. Property values in the city have sky-rocketed, leaving an Englishman who thought himself the owner of quite a decent little residence feeling very much the poor relation, while a 20-year old wishing to run a car in Dublin may well have to pay something around €3,500 each year in insurance. Dublin has grown and grown, the roads have become more and more congested, and, perhaps somewhat belatedly, there has been a realisation that only public transport can prevent gridlock. It has even been quite seriously suggested that Dublin could grow at such a rate that it might become another Los Angeles, swallowing up the surrounding countryside with vast housing and commercial developments and a road network to match.

The DART has more than proved its worth, passenger numbers having doubled since its inauguration. Equally revolutionary, and also likely to prove an invaluable asset, is the LUAS tram network. Two routes opened in the summer of 2004, the Green Line, much of it over the old Harcourt Street line, from Sandyford to St Stephen's Green, and the Red Line, from Tallaght to Connolly. Built by Alsthom SA, the Green Line trams are five-section articulated vehicles, the Red Line ones being very similar three-section cars. Although the two systems are presently separate, a new Minister for Transport, Martin Cullen TD, announced in November 2004 that he intended to see them connected with a line through the heart of the city within two years.

LUAS has been extraordinarily successful, despite a number of relatively minor accidents, caused by motorists ignoring red lights giving the trams right of way. A report at the end of 2004 commented that, unlike tram systems everywhere else, there was reluctance on the part of a small number of Dublin motorists to respect the right of way of the tram.

Nearly half a million passengers were carried during the first five days of the opening of the Sandyford line in July 2004, and both routes carry some 20,000 passengers each day. They bring people in from the suburbs infinitely faster than any other means of transport, with none of the frustration of driving a car. The next ten years is going to be perhaps the most exciting period ever for rail travel in its various forms in and around Dublin as the various networks extend and take the strain of carrying the ever-growing number of commuters, shoppers, visitors, schoolchildren, students and others in and around one of Europe's most vibrant capitals.

Finally, a word of warning to the unwary. In 1966, to commemorate the 50th anniversary of the 1916 uprising that led to the independence of the 26 Counties, the three Dublin termini were renamed, Amiens Street becoming Connolly, Kingsbridge becoming Heuston, and Westland Row becoming Pearse. Older citizens still often use the original names, but in the captions whichever was current at the time that each photograph was taken has been used.

Michael H. C. Baker
Wareham, Dorset

Greystones and Bray

GREYSTONES has traditionally been regarded as the southern-most extremity of the Dublin suburban area, although perhaps not all the residents would agree. In the first view push-pull set No 6106 stands in Greystones station ready to depart for Bray in early 1984. From 1984 until 1990 the Greystones shuttle operated a very good service, between 15 and 20 trains doing the spectacular 11-minute journey in each direction along the cliffs between Bray and Greystones. The service was worked at first by a push-pull set, later by a diesel-electric multiple unit (DEMU) hired from Northern Ireland Railways. Outside rush hours it was not terribly well patronised, and when the NIR set was returned north in November 1990, the shuttle, despite much local protest, came to an end, and the service was reduced to no more than eight up and six down passenger trains calling at Greystones Halt, as it was then classed in the working timetable.

In August 1993 the Shelton Abbey Sidings (north of Arklow) to Marino Point, Cork, ammonia empties, headed by General Motors 141 Class Bo-Bo No 152, passes the stock of the Railway Preservation Society of Ireland 'Sea Breeze' special from Dublin to Rosslare.

The population of the Greystones area continues to grow, and has been part of the DART system since April 2000. One of the original 1984 German-built units is about to depart for the city in July 2004. *All MHCB*

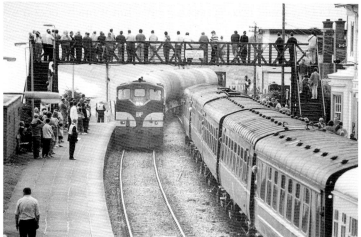

BRAY: The 10.00am Westland Row to Wexford train climbs out of Bray behind former Dublin & South Eastern Railway (CIE 'J8' Class) 0-6-0 No 445, built in 1905.

The 18.30 Dublin Connolly (Amiens Street until renamed in 1966) to Rosslare train is seen at the same spot on a very wet August evening in 1996 hauled by General Motors 071 Class 2,250hp Co-Co No 082. *Neil Sprinks/MHCB*

Swinging the camera in the other direction we see an up train rounding the curve into Bray behind a rebuilt former Great Southern & Western Railway (GSWR) '333' Class 4-4-0 around 1930. *Author's collection*

BRAY: The down platform at Bray in Great Southern days. Some time around 1930 No 539, a 4-4-0 built by the Midland Great Western Railway (MGWR) at Broadstone in 1910 and classified 'D7' by the GSR, has charge of two arc-roofed corridors.

In December 1995 a DART from Howth arrives at the down platform while another prepares to head north from the up platform during the evening rush hour. The lights of the city can just be seen over the station roof on either side of the tall multi-chimneyed building to the right. *Author's collection/MHCB*

BRAY is a seaside town that benefited enormously from the arrival of the railway in 1854; indeed, it could lay claim to being Ireland's premier resort. As the 19th century progressed so it became equally popular as a residential area, the journey into Dublin being accomplished within the hour. Today, as with so many resorts close to great cities – one thinks of Bangor in the North, New Brighton on the Mersey estuary, Southend at the mouth of the Thames – the holiday traffic has dwindled as commuting has grown.

In later steam days practically any class of locomotive, apart from a 4-6-0, might be seen on the coast line south of Dublin. One of the regular performers is seen in the first picture, former Cork, Bandon & South Coast 4-6-0T No 466, built

by Beyer Peacock in 1920 and hauling the 11.20 am to Dublin Amiens Street on 20 March 1954.

The second view, dating from September 1967, shows Metropolitan-Vickers Co-Co No A13 of 1955 with its original Crossley 1,200hp engine about to depart for Dublin Connolly with a returning evening rush-hour train.

Moving on to 1971, with Bray Head in the background, one of the pioneer General Motors Bo-Bos of 1961, No B132, stands ready to depart with a Rosslare to Dublin express on 11 September. At the opposite platform preserved former GSWR 'J15' Class 0-6-0 No 186 stands at the head of a Railway Preservation Society of Ireland (RPSI) rail tour.

Finally we see three DARTs at the same location on 2 January 1996. *Author's collection/MHCB/Ron Elsdon/MHCB*

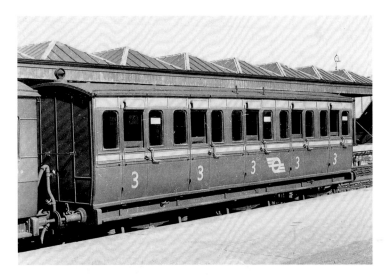

Above BRAY: As varied as the locomotive stock was the coaching collection. In the 1950s anything from an ancient six-wheeler to the latest wide-bodied all-steel Bulleid designs were commonplace on the Bray to Dublin commuter trains. No 30M, a six-wheel, five-compartment 3rd built at Broadstone in 1895, stands at the up platform on 23 June 1952. *Neil Sprinks*

Above right This variety persisted beyond steam days and almost until electrification. This is a close-up of a compartment of No 898, a ten-compartment non-corridor bogie 3rd built at Inchicore in 1907 and seen at Bray in the summer of 1971. Note the low-backed seats, the matchboard compartment walls, the leather strap for the droplight, and the gas lamp fittings in the arc roof. *MHCB*

Above This extraordinary collection of four-wheelers, seen at Bray in the summer of 1978, was built for the Sean Connery/Donald Sutherland film *The First Great Train Robbery*. Replicas of English South Eastern Railway carriages of the 1850s, I watched them being loaded on to road wagons for storage at the nearby Ardmore Studios, where for all I know they may still be. In the distance a 201 Class Bo-Bo is approaching with a Greystones-Dublin Connolly train, passing the locomotive shed and imposing bracket signal. MHCB

BRAY: A train of Edwardian non-corridor carriages disgorges day-trippers on August Bank Holiday Sunday, 1970, while a rather less animated group of commuters stands at the same spot one August morning in 1994. *Both MHCB*

BRAY: In the first picture No 61, an ancient Ivatt '60' ('D14') Class 4-4-0, complete with outside-frame tender, built at Inchicore in 1891, arrives at Bray with the 12.53pm from Amiens Street on 20 March 1954. A railcar, newly in service, waits in the siding on the extreme left of the picture.

Pulling out of Bray for Dublin with the 9.20 am from Rosslare on the same day is No 339, a rather more modern former GSWR 4-4-0. With its 5ft 8½in driving wheels and unusual outside-framed bogie reminiscent of GWR practice, No 339 was built in 1908 especially for the Rosslare road. Its load of one modern CIE carriage, one GSWR bogie and a van is hardly taxing.

The third photograph is a view from the footbridge seen in the two previous pictures. An A Class Co-Co leaves Bray with a Dublin Connolly train in August 1969.

Finally we see a DART curving away from Bray in December 1995. Just visible over the trees are the smoking chimneys of the Pigeon House power station at the mouth of the Liffey, while somewhere in the trees is the site of Shanganah Junction, where the Harcourt Street branch left the main coast line. *Neil Sprinks (2)/MHCB (2)*

BRAY: A scene outside the engine shed at the country end of Bray station at the turn of the century. Nearest the camera are two of the long-lived Sharp Stewart 0-4-2s built for the Dublin, Wicklow & Wexford Railway in 1864, the further one being No 22, which was withdrawn in 1910.

The commuter service between Bray and Howth was electrified in 1984. The 'present' photograph shows a Linke-Hofmann-Busch/GEC DART EMU, driving trailer car No 8309, standing outside the wall of the shed in December 1995. *Author's collection/MHCB*

Harcourt Street

Above SHANGANAH JUNCTION is seen looking towards Dublin. It was here that the two routes into the city, the coast line to Westland Row and Amiens Street and the inland one to Harcourt Street, diverged. *Adrian Vaughan collection*

Below STILLORGAN station, now a private house, was photographed in August 1996. The fence in the foreground marks the boundary of Brewery Road, which passes over what used to be the bridge over the railway. *MHCB*

STILLORGAN: A special from Harcourt Street to Foxrock for Leopardstown Races passes Stillorgan on 20 March 1954. The train consists of ten six-wheelers and one bogie carriage, while the engine, No 717, is one of the not very successful 'J15Bs', a 1935-built supposed improvement on the immensely successful 'J15s' built between 1866 and 1903. The Harcourt Street line was closed in 1958, and the trackbed returned to nature.

The long awaited revival of the Harcourt Street line finally came to fruition on 30 June 2004 with the inauguration of the LUAS tram system. The once rural area of Stillorgan and Sandyford, transformed into a state-of-the-art 21st-century business and residential district demanded a 21st-century solution to its traffic problems. The result is the 770-million-Euro LUAS, which has brought Stillorgan just 20 minutes from the city centre. The most spectacular feature of the revived line is the 9-million-Euro bridge at Dundrum. A public competition resulted in it being named the Dargan Bridge after William J. Dargan (1799-1867), the Father of Irish Railways. This is a view from a tram speeding across the Dargan Bridge on its way to Stillorgan in July 2004. *Neil Sprinks/MHCB*

Above HARCOURT STREET station is seen in about 1950. The engine on the left, No 660, is a former MGWR 'G2' Class 2-4-0, built in 1894, that on the right, No 63, a former GSWR 'D14' 4-4-0 of 1891. On the extreme right is one of the Drumm battery trains, Dublin's first encounter with electric

Below and right Harcourt Street station as seen from the street in August 1996. Like all Dublin termini, it was a good deal more impressive without than within. The platforms ran parallel to the street and the office blocks on the right of the picture stand more or less where the trains did in the previous picture. After closure the station was sold in 1959 as offices for £67,500, the largest amount then ever paid at an auction for property in Dublin. New LUAS tram No 4007 pauses outside. *Both MHCB*

21

Left HARCOURT STREET: One of the principal reasons why the original Harcourt Street line closed was the distance of its terminus from the city centre, but now the LUAS system comes right down Harcourt Street, into St Stephen's Green and terminates at the top of Grafton Street, which is said to be the 'fourth most expensive shopping street in the world'. One of the shopping malls opposite the LUAS terminus saw its trade increase by 25% in the first weeks of tram operations. Shoppers get ready to board tram No 4014 as it reaches the St Stephen's Green terminus on 27 December 2004, the first day of the sales. *MHCB*

BANK OF IRELAND AND TRINITY COLLEGE, DUBLIN.   R.556

Middle and bottom Trams used, of course, to be a familiar sight in Dublin, and in this view of the Bank of Ireland and Trinity College in the 1930s there are four four-wheelers (bogie cars were also used), with an AEC Regal single-deck bus in the foreground on route 54 heading for Kimmage Crossroads. The last Dublin tram ran in 1949.

The second picture shows the same junction in August 1996. The notion of sight-seeing city tours in an open-top double-deck would have seemed pretty far-fetched in the 1930s, but as in so many modern cities today they are an essential tourist attraction. D710, a Van Hool-bodied Leyland Atlantean, seems to be doing pretty good business. *Author's collection/MHCB*

Through Killiney

KILLINEY: An A Class Co-Co is seen south of Killiney station with the 17.52 from Dublin Connolly on the last leg of its journey to Bray in August 1969. Bray Head is in the distance.

In August 1993 an 001, a re-engined A Class, passes the same location with the 18.30 Connolly to Rosslare train. In the intervening 24 years housing estates have sprung up in profusion so that there is now virtually no open countryside between Bray and Dublin. *Both MHCB*

24

Opposite page KILLINEY: The section between Killiney and Dalkey is probably the most famous stretch of railway line in Ireland, running as it does along the cliff edge above Dublin Bay and beneath some of the finest and most exclusive residences in the country, homes of ambassadors, pop stars, writers and the like. On a very clear day it is possible to see the mountains of Wales from the top of Killiney Hill. The 'past' view shows No B227 in charge of a Bray-bound push-pull as it drifts down the hill above a crowded Killiney beach in August 1976, while looking south in 1996 a DART approaches the same location. *Both MHCB*

This page KILLINEY: The first of these two further 'past' views of traffic along the coast line shows an eight-car railcar set, forming a Rosslare to Dublin Amiens Street train, climbing towards the summit in the mid-1950s, while in the second, some ten years later, General Motors (GM) Bo-Bo No B168 has charge of an up demonstration train at the same spot. *Both author's collection*

25

Above **DALKEY: The first electric trams in Dublin started running between Dalkey and Ballsbridge on 16 May 1896, and this picture, taken in Castle Street, Dalkey, shows four-wheel double-deck car No 285 shortly after entering service in 1901. The railway immediately felt the competition, but it would be over 80 years before its own electrification schemes came about.**
  In December 1995 Castle Street is surprisingly little changed, except for the traffic of course. *W. Lawrence/MHCB*

Right **Equally surprising is the fact that the tram tracks leading out of Castle Street into Dalkey Depot still exist, as do the initials of Dublin Corporation Tramways on the iron gates.** *Both MHCB*

GLENAGEARY: Work is in preparation for the DART in December 1982, and the completed electrification is seen in August 1996. *Both MHCB*

Kingstown/Dun Laoghaire

Above and right DUN LAOGHAIRE: On 13 July 1957 the main line is still single track, and the Carlisle Pier branch can be seen diverging to the right. Above is the station building, by this time converted to a cafe.

At the same scene in August 1996 the branch has gone and the double track is laid on a concrete base. The delightful ornate iron shelter has been refurbished and the former station building has now moved up market to become a superior fish restaurant. *Author's collection/MHCB*

Below A 1983 photograph showing the new slab track in the cutting alongside the promenade at Dun Laoghaire in preparation for electrification. The recently lifted line to Carlisle Pier used to curve away in the short tunnel to the left. *MHCB*

DUN LAOGHAIRE: Carlisle Pier, Kingstown (as Dun Laoghaire was known until independence), had been the terminus of boat trains since 1857. It was a most convenient arrangement – one simply stepped (or possibly staggered) off the boat and into the train, or vice versa. No 637, one of the MGWR's last 0-6-0s, a 'J5' dating from 1922, makes no effort to slip away quietly in about 1955 with the London, Midland & Scottish Railway-designed mail boat *Cambria* tied up alongside.

On a damp August evening in 1981 a 201 Class Bo-Bo is about to set off with the boat train for Pearse. The Sealink ferry *St Columba*, successor to the *Cambria* and *Hibernia*, is alongside.

The Carlisle Pier line closed in 1980 when the DART system was inaugurated. In August 1996, although the *St Columba*, latterly the *Hibernia*, now renamed *Stena Adventurer*, still operates, most passengers, whether on foot, in motor coaches or in their cars, now travel by the Stena Line *HSS* catamaran seen loading up on the opposite side of the harbour. Carlisle Pier is now disused, and there are ambitious plans to demolish it and replace it with an extensive multi-storey office, apartment and shopping development. Not surprisingly this is highly controversial and has roused considerable opposition. *Adrian Vaughan collection/MHCB (2)*

Holyhead-Dun Laoghaire

The low cost, short cut to Ireland

May 5 1975 to October 5 1975

Inter-City ⤧ Sealink

DUN LAOGHAIRE: The 5,284 gross ton mail boat *Cambria*, ordered by the LMS from Harland & Wolff and delivered to British Railways in 1948, enters Dun Laoghaire harbour on a calm August evening in 1969. Howth can be seen in the background. *MHCB*

The *Stena Hibernia*, the 1977 successor to the *Cambria* and her sister ship the earlier *Hibernia*, at Dun Laoghaire in August 1993. *MHCB*

An astonishing new shape appeared on the Irish Sea in 1995. The Stena Sealink *Stena Sea Lynx* arrives at Dun Laoghaire on a deceptively calm morning in December 1995. A few days later I spent 24¼ hours on the *Hibernia*, most of it within sight of Holyhead waiting for the east wind to subside. This comfortably beat my previous record of 17 hours in an Irish Sea gale. The irony of this is that we had transferred our booking from the *Lynx* because it didn't sail in gale force winds. *MHCB*

By the summer of 1996 the astonishing Stena Line (Sealink had by now been dropped from the title) *HSS*, built in Finland and claimed to be the largest catamaran in the world, had taken over the Holyhead-Dun Laoghaire run. Scheduled to complete the journey in just under 2 hours, it initially created a wash of such ferocity in Dublin Bay that its effects took half an hour to subside and it had to operate at reduced speed until clear of the Kish lighthouse. *MHCB*

DUN LAOGHAIRE: No 674, an 'I3' 0-6-2T dating from 1933 and one of only 29 engines built by the Great Southern Railway, stands at Dun Laoghaire with a down train in June 1956.

In the second view CIE 550hp Bo-Bo No C221, still in its original wildly impractical silver livery, is seen at Dun Laoghaire shortly after delivery from the Metro-Cammell works in Manchester in 1957. It is standing under the then recently erected concrete footbridge.

Northbound and southbound DARTs pass at Dun Laoghaire in July 2004. The further train is one of the original 81xx series, the nearer a Japanese Tokyu 8510 Class delivered during 2004. *Neil Sprinks/Kevin Murray/MHCB*

DUN LAOGHAIRE: No 339, a former GSWR 'D4' Class 4-4-0 built at Inchicore in 1907, heads an up train at Dun Laoghaire in 1957. The up platform, on the right, is under construction and will be completed later that year; in the meantime all stopping trains use the one platform. The third and fourth carriages are brand-new 10ft 2in-wide 76-seat unpainted suburban composites built by Park Royal.

The second view shows the station shortly after the DART inauguration in July 1984. A DART occupies the space vacated by the 'D4' and its train of 27 years before. *Kevin Murray/MHCB*

DUN LAOGHAIRE: Former Dublin & South Eastern Railway (DSER) 'C3' Class 4-4-2T No 460, built by Sharp Stewart in 1893, arrives at Dun Laoghaire with the 12.38pm from Amiens Street, consisting of four six-wheelers and two bogie carriages, on 5 June 1954, while the 'present' view shows an early morning DART departure in August 1996. *Neil Sprinks/MHCB*

DUN LAOGHAIRE: Former GSWR 'D14' Class 4-4-0 No 62 of 1891 leaves Dun Laoghaire with the 9.20am Rosslare Harbour-Westland Row train on 5 June 1954.

What was once the rather grand entrance to Dun Laoghaire station, or rather Kingstown as it was originally, facing the harbour, has for many years now been an up-market fish restaurant. *Neil Sprinks/MHCB*

DUN LAOGHAIRE: One of the last 'J15s', No 254 of 1903, with a superheated boiler, approaches Dun Laoghaire from the north with the then usual rake of ancient and modern bogie carriages in June 1956.

Forty years later a DART passes the harbour, which is now full of dinghies and various other sailing vessels. *Neil Sprinks/*MHCB

Looking in the opposite direction, two of the original 121 Class GM Bo-Bos of 1961, No 123 leading, pass the same location with a Rosslare-Dublin train in August 1986. *MHCB*

Westland Row/Pearse and Tara Street

BOOTERSTOWN: No 2639, one of the AEC/Park Royal railcars introduced in 1951 (this one dates from 1953), speeds through the disused Booterstown station at the head of the 12.52 Connolly-Bray service on 9 April 1971.

Twenty-four years later years later Booterstown station has been re-opened, and a DART approaches in December 1995. *Ron Elsdon/MHCB*

Comparisons of the interiors of one of the former Park Royal railcars converted to push-pull operation (*above*) and a DART. *Both MHCB*

LANSDOWNE ROAD: On 16 April 1971 GM Bo-Bo No B177 has charge of the 17.27 Dalkey-Dundalk train. The leading vehicle is one of the four-wheel heating vans introduced in 1957.

A southbound six-coach DART, with driving trailer No 8628 of a Tokyu four-car unit leading and a two-car Alsthom Spanish-built 8200 series trailing, heads under the stands of Lansdowne Road stadium as it approaches the station on 28 December 2004. *Ron Elsdon/MHCB*

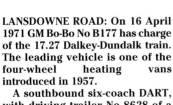

BALLSBRIDGE: Metro-Vickers Bo-Bo No C214 stands at the head of a line of cattle wagons on the Royal Dublin Society siding at Ballsbridge in August 1969. This was a special that had brought horses for the famous Dublin Horse Show, and this must have been about the last year that any competitors arrived by rail.

The site is quite unrecognisable now, the line having been removed and the whole area redeveloped as bank and insurance office headquarters. *Both MHCB*

GRAND CANAL STREET: Two DSER locomotives stand beside the gasworks at Grand Canal Street. No 445, a 'J8' Class 0-6-0 built by Beyer Peacock for the DSER, was photographed on 18 June 1938, while the picture of No 462 dates from 15 May 1950. No 462 was one of the two DSER Beyer Peacock 2-6-0s built in 1922; her number appears to be chalked on. Withdrawn and broken up in 1963, her sister, No 461, has been preserved and features several times in these pages.

Always a striking feature of the approach to Dublin, the gasworks had fallen out of use by the 1990s. However, rather like those between King's Cross and St Pancras stations in London, their importance as a piece of industrial heritage has been recognised, and although the left-hand gas-holder was in the process of being demolished when I took this picture of a DART passing in April 1994, the nearer, more ornate one has been preserved. By the beginning of 2005 an astonishing transformation was taking place: within the framework of the former gasholder was being built a complex of apartments in what is fast becoming a highly desirable area of the city. *Henry Casserley (2)/MHCB*

GRAND CANAL STREET SHED: The now preserved former DSER 2-6-0 No 461 simmers away in the June sunshine outside Grand Canal Street shed in 1938. *Henry Casserley*

No 291, an archaic-looking 2-4-0 built by Dubs for the Waterford, Limerick & Western Railway in 1893 and christened Nephin, finds itself far from home at Grand Canal Street shortly before its withdrawal in 1959. *Kevin Murray*

Grand Canal Dock station now stands more or less opposite the site of the steam shed, built to serve the huge number of offices and apartments springing up here, a graphic illustration of the 'Celtic Tiger' that has seen the Republic of Ireland transformed in the last couple of decades from one of Europe's poorest countries into one of its richest. *MHCB*

GRAND CANAL STREET: Looking south now, we see a line of 4-4-0s at Grand Canal Street in 1953, being serviced prior to returning with specials that have brought GAA enthusiasts to Dublin. *Kevin Murray*

'G2' Class 2-4-0 No 660 has charge of a diesel railcar set that appears to be in difficulties beside the sidings at Grand Canal Street in about 1953. Stock for Westland Row station was stabled here. The 'G2', a Midland Great Western design dating from 1893, was the longest-lived 2-4-0 in these islands, the last one not being withdrawn until 1963. *Kevin Murray*

Suburban stock being shunted at the Grand Canal Street sidings in July 1979. In the distance a push-pull set is approaching from Bray, overtaking a 201 Class Bo-Bo. *MHCB*

Opposite WESTLAND ROW/PEARSE: This is the view from Pearse station looking back towards Grand Canal Street in August 1969. The locomotive is one of the recently rebuilt A Class of 1956, while the carriage on the extreme left is No 1115, a bogie brake van built by the GSWR in 1912 and, when withdrawn in 1973, the last arc-roofed coach in ordinary main-line service in the British Isles.

In the March 1994 view the locomotives are Irish Rail GM 950hp single-cab Bo-Bos, built in 1961. The one on the right is standing at the head of a push-pull outer suburban set. Gone is the signal box spanning the tracks, and prominent is the catenary for the DART electrics. *Both MHCB*

This page WESTLAND ROW/PEARSE: On Christmas Eve 1979 a GM 141 Class Bo-Bo pulls out of Pearse with the 11.42 Howth to Greystones train. At the same location in August 1996 is one of the 201 Class Co-Co locomotives, No 229 *Abhainn na Mainge/River Maine*, pulling into the station from the sidings with the 12.25 to Drogheda consisting of a six-coach push-pull unit dating from 1989. Built at La Grange, Illinois, and introduced in 1994/5, the 32 members of the class have a nominal 3,000 traction horsepower, making then the most powerful locomotives yet seen in Ireland. All are named after rivers, one nameplate being in English, the other in Gaelic. *Both MHCB*

WESTLAND ROW/PEARSE: No B218 is about to leave Pearse with a Dun Laoghaire boat train in August 1972. The leading carriage is of GNR origin. Heading north from the station in August 1996 is a Howth-bound DART. *Both MHCB*

WESTLAND ROW/PEARSE: A boat train from Dun Laoghaire has just arrived on 28 July 1971. Today the terminal platform 5 at which it is standing is no longer used for passenger traffic.

In August 1996 a DART stands at platform 4. Although not immediately obvious, the high arched roof, the only such example in Dublin, has been completely refurbished with new glazing and glazing bars, making it much lighter and the appearance of the station much brighter. *Ron Elsdon/MHCB*

WESTLAND ROW/PEARSE: A DART approaches Pearse station in August 1996. Although Pearse is pretty central, Tara Street, some 400 yards distant and hidden by the trees immediately to the right of the DART, is even more so. *MHCB*

TARA STREET: Westland Row used to be the starting point for main-line trains to the west, and in the first picture 'K1' Class 'Mogul' No 378 accelerates through Tara Street with the 8.40am to Galway on 30 May 1953. No 378 was a Maunsell design, virtually identical to his SECR and Southern Railway engines; built at the Woolwich Arsenal during the First World War, they were bought as a set of parts by the MGWR and re-assembled in Dublin. There were 26 in all and, apart from performing many other duties, they were the principal passenger engines on the Midland main lines until replaced by diesels.

The second view (*opposite above*) shows 'J15' No 256 arriving at Tara Street tender-first with the 8.52am Dun Laoghaire-Amiens Street train on the same day.

The 'present' photograph (*opposite below*) is of GM Bo-Bo No 182 passing through Tara Street in August 1996 with Shelton to Marino Point ammonia empties. *Neil Sprinks (2)/MHCB*

TARA STREET: 'C2' No 456, a former DSER 4-4-2T dating from 1924, comes off the Liffey Viaduct as it pulls into Tara Street from the north with a suburban train on 30 May 1953.

In April 1994 two GM Bo-Bos, No 187 leading, have charge of the Marino Point-Shelton ammonia train as they cross the Liffey. The line is now dominated by the overhead catenary for the DART and the 1960s-built Liberty Hall, headquarters of the Irish Trade Union movement and the tallest building in Dublin. *Neil Sprinks/MHCB*

Amiens Street/Connolly

AMIENS STREET/CONNOLLY: The 17.52 to Bray stands at platform 6 at Connolly in 1969. The train is made up of what was by then the oldest vehicles in regular main-line use within the British Isles, six-compartment, wooden-bodied carriages built by the GSWR, the two oldest being arc-roofed, gas-lit 3rds dating from 1907/9.

A series of wide-bodied, lightweight carriages constructed with parts supplied by Park Royal at Inchicore was put into suburban service in 1955, the last not being withdrawn until the mid-1990s. Here one stands at the head of an Arklow-bound train behind an 001 Co-Co while a DART approaches in the distance in August 1990. *Both MHCB*

AMIENS STREET/CONNOLLY: One of the most adventurous innovations on the railway systems within these islands in the 1930s was the Drumm battery train. Dr Drumm was a professor at University College, Dublin, and he and his team of scientists developed a revolutionary type of battery that was tried out by the Great Southern Railway. This two-car unit, B, was the second of four built between 1932 and 1939. Able to work 80 miles before it needed recharging, it is seen here at Amiens Street in 1938 about to depart for Bray. The units lasted until 1949-50 when electric traction disappeared from the Dublin suburban system until the DARTs appeared 34 years later.

Standing at the same platform around 1950 in the second picture is a former DSER 'C2' 4-4-2T.

In the summer of 1986 rebuilt Metro-Vickers Co-Co No 034 stands at the same platform alongside a Bray-bound DART. The footbridge, which spanned both GNR and GSR tracks, was removed and replaced by a subway, and new awnings were erected with the arrival of the DART in 1984. *Author's collection (2)/MHCB*

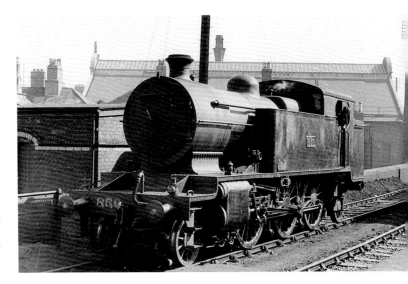

Swinging the camera round we see No 850, the solitary 'P1' Class 2-6-2T built by the GSR for Dublin suburban traffic in 1928; the photograph was taken in 1938. *Henry Casserley*

AMIENS STREET/CONNOLLY: Four views of the former DSER/GSR side at the north end of Amiens Street/Connolly. The first shows the station in early GSR days; a 4-4-2T stands on the turntable on the right.

In the second picture, taken on 20 March 1954, Maunsell 'Mogul' No 373 passes the GSR-built signal box with the 8.40am Westland Row to Galway train.

On 28 May 1955 No 624, one of the big 'J5' Class 0-6-0s built by the MGWR in 1924, pulls away with a Midland line train.

The fourth view shows the empty stock of a Sligo train and a DART in December 1996.

In the final view an Iarnrod Eireann maintenance vehicle stands on the turntable on 19 December 2004. *Author's collection/ Neil Sprinks (2)/MHCB (2)*

This page AMIENS STREET/CONNOLLY: Inside Amiens Street station in the early 1920s is No 57, a 'J10' Class Tri-composite Brake built for the GNR in the early years of the century.

In August 1974 the 'Enterprise', composed of CIE-built Craven carriages dating from the 1960s, has just arrived at Connolly from Belfast. *Author's collection/MHCB*

Opposite page AMIENS STREET/CONNOLLY: A GNR 'B' Class 0-6-0 of 1877/9 shunts a handsome clerestory non-corridor 3rd at Amiens Street on 29 May 1955.

Fourteen years later, in August 1969, shunting is being carried out by 400hp CIE shunter No E425. Two GSWR arc-roofed carriages dated from about 1906 are in the sidings behind. *Neil Sprinks/MHCB*

AMIENS STREET/CONNOLLY: English railway historians, particularly those addicted to the Great Western Railway, often forget how much to the forefront Ireland was in developing the diesel railcar between the wars, none more so than the GNR. Railcar G, seen in the first photograph, was a two-car articulated unit powered by a Gardner 102hp engine powering a central bogie, which actually made it three vehicles, the central section being mounted over the power bogie. Here it enters Amiens Street on 29 May 1955.

In the second photograph GNR 'U' Class 4-4-0 No 197 *Lough Neagh* enters the station with a train from Drogheda on 8 September 1959. The Great Northern Railway (Ireland) had ceased to exist at midnight on 30 September of the previous year, hence the 'CIE' stencilled on the buffer beam, although Lough Neagh retains her beautiful, and very well maintained, lined blue livery complete with GNR crest on the tender. The first two carriages have been repainted in CIE green.

Looking north from the other side of Connolly in August 1974, a CIE 201 Class Bo-Bo shunts a train of one four-wheeled heating van, five Park Royals and a wooden-bodied suburban Brake 3rd built by the GSR in the mid 1920s.

With the removal of the footbridge it is not possible to exactly replicate the earlier pictures, but this ground-level view is taken from approximately the same position on 19 December 2004. From left to right are one of the original 1984 DARTs, a Class 2900 railcar, a 141 Class GM Bo-Bo, and 201 Class 3,000hp Co-Co No 228, newly repainted into a most attractive livery of yellow, green and silver. *Neil Sprinks/MHCB (3)*

AMIENS STREET/CONNOLLY: In the first of these three views, a four-car unit headed by No 614, an AEC/Park Royal diesel railcar introduced in 1950, pulls out of Amiens Street on an excursion working in May 1955. In the distance the 'Bundoran Express' waits to depart.

The last diesel railcars built for the GNR were 24 vehicles of BUT/Dundalk construction that entered service between June 1957 and October 1958. They were subsequently divided up between CIE and NIR, and one of the 701-17 series with corridor connections at both ends (below left) stands in the 'Howth Bay' platform at Connolly at the head of a six-car NIR Belfast-bound train in August 1970.

In the 'present' view (*opposite top*) a 8200 series DART arrives at Connolly station from Howth on 19 December 2004. *Neil Sprinks/MHCB (2)*

Above A general view of both sides of Connolly station looking south towards the city centre in August 1972. One the far left is No E430, a Maybach-engined 400hp diesel-hydraulic shunter of 1961, ahead of No 2509, a Gardner/Walker diesel railcar built for the Sligo, Leitrim & Northern Counties Railway in 1947 and bought by CIE when this closed down. Behind again is a re-engined A Class Co-Co, a varied collection of GSWR, GSR, GNR and CIE-built carriages, and another E Class shunter. AEC/Park Royal railcar No 2644 pulls out past the GNR-built signal box with a northbound stopping train. *MHCB*

Right The Great Northern Railway went out of existence in 1958, but remarkably this notice was still intact and in almost pristine condition at Connolly station in August 1996. *MHCB*

Opposite AMIENS STREET/CONNOLLY: The GNR was famous for its many series of 4-4-0s, ranging from small branch-line engines to powerful express locomotives designed specifically for the Dublin-Belfast main line. Five 'V' Class three-cylinder compounds were introduced by Glover in 1932. Originally painted black, they were repainted in a wonderful sky blue livery with black and white lining, which they retained until withdrawal between 1959 and 1963. No 83 *Eagle* pulls out of Amiens Street with a Belfast express soon after acquiring blue livery. No 85 *Merlin* has been preserved in working order and can still be seen from time to time at Connolly.

The very last new class of 4-4-0 in Europe, probably in the world, was built in Manchester by Beyer Peacock for the GNR in 1948. This was the three-cylinder simple version of the 'Vs', the 'VS'. Like the 'Vs' there were five of them, this time named after Irish rivers. No 210 *Erne* pulls out of Amiens Street with a Belfast express on 29 May 1955. *Author's collection/Neil Sprinks*

This page AMIENS STREET/CONNOLLY: Diesel railcars took up regular work on the Dublin-Belfast main line as early as 1950, but steam was not finally ousted until late 1966. In 1970 three Bo-Bo 1,350hp diesel-electric locomotives were built by English Electric/BREL/Hunslet for the Dublin-Belfast 'Enterprise' expresses; at the same time a fleet of BR Mark IIb carriages were delivered from the Derby works of British Rail Engineering, source of so many carriages for the former Northern Counties Committee (NCC) of the LMS. The three locomotives were given bird names formerly carried by the compound 4-4-0s, and here No 101 *Eagle* stands ready to depart from Connolly in August 1970 alongside a rake of GNR carriages repainted in CIE orange and black livery.

The latest locomotives to take up work between Dublin and Belfast are the 3,000hp General Motors Co-Cos, delivery of which began in June 1994. The first 112-tonne locomotive was flown across the Atlantic in a Russian Antonov 124, the world's largest cargo aircraft, stopping off at Reykjavik – thereby briefly bringing the total of railway locomotives in that country to three, its highest ever! Like the GNR 'VS' 4-4-0s, they are named after Irish rivers, the nameplate on one side being in Irish, the other in English. No 232 *Abhainn na Chomaraigh/River Cummeragh* is about to depart from Connolly with the 0755 to Belfast on 23 December 1995. *Both MHCB*

AMIENS STREET DEPOT: Blue-liveried GNR 'S' Class 4-4-0 No 174 *Carrantouhill* stands outside Amiens Street depot on 7 September 1961. The five 'S' Class engines were built in 1913-15; extensively rebuilt in the late 1930s, they were considered by many to be the equals of the compounds. All five lasted until 1964/5; No 171 *Slieve Gullion* was taken into preservation and, except for periods of overhaul, has now been active on the Dublin-Belfast main line, as well as many other routes both sides of the border, for over 80 years. *MHCB*

The Northern Counties Committee of the LMS ordered 18 2-6-4Ts immediately after the Second World War, and this 'WT' Class proved to be the last steam engines in ordinary service in Ireland, some working the Dublin-Belfast route in their later years. No 4 has been preserved and is seen here at Connolly depot preparing to work back to Belfast on 1 September 1984. *MHCB*

In the foreground outside Connolly depot in December 1995 is Irish Rail 141 Class 875hp Bo-Bo No 171, next to 071 Class 2,250hp Co-Co No 074; arriving with the 0900 service from Belfast is NIR 111 Class Co-Co (identical to the IR 071s) No 112 *Northern Counties*. *MHCB*

To Howth and Malahide

Above and right EAST WALL JUNCTION is just over half a mile north of Connolly station, and the line seen here curving away to the left leads to North Wall and the extensive goods yards there. CIE AEC/Park Royal railcar No 2650 heads a Connolly-Drogheda stopping train in the summer of 1970.

In the second photograph the junction is seen from a southbound express in August 1996. *Both MHCB*

Below Looking towards the junction from the North Wall line, a 201 Class Bo-Bo propels a Howth-bound push-pull set in August 1975. Plenty of GNR wooden-post, lower-quadrant semaphore signals are in evidence. *MHCB*

Above and right EAST WALL JUNCTION: Immediately north of East Wall Junction box the GNR main line crosses the River Tolka. Normally a placid little stream, it flooded to such an extent in 1954 that it carried away the railway bridge; on 28 May 1955 'VS' 4-4-0 No 207 *Boyne* heads gingerly across the temporary bridge with a Belfast-bound express. East Wall Junction signal box in seen in the left distance.

The 'present' view was taken in August 1996 from the 1700 Belfast-Connolly train, crossing the reinforced concrete bridge that now spans the river. *Neil Sprinks/MHCB*

Below FAIRVIEW: In the late 1950s a depot for railcars was built at Fairview, just north of the Tolka Bridge. This was later replaced by the present DART depot. In August 1994 NIR Co-Co No 112 *Northern Counties* accelerates past DARTs in the depot with the 1300 Dublin to Belfast 'Enterprise'. *MHCB*

66

In August 1978 the 1730 Connolly to Belfast train is propelled passed the depot by NIR Bo-Bo No 101 *Eagle*. The complete train has just been repainted in a livery of grey and blue. *MHCB*

This wider view shows the handsome GNR East Wall Junction signal box, the river bridge and depot, and CIE 201 Class Bo-Bo No 231 standing on the down main line in August 1982. *MHCB*

This page FAIRVIEW: On 29 May 1955 GNR 'S' Class 4-4-0 No 173 *Galtee More* accelerates the 8.45am 'Bundoran Express' away from Amiens Street; it will travel by way of Dundalk, Clones and Enniskillen to the little County Donegal resort.

By August 1971 the depot has appeared on the right, and the land to the left skirting Dublin Bay, which in 1955 would have been under water at high tide, has been partly reclaimed. No 2600, CIE's first railcar and originally used on long-distance main-line work, heads north with a Connolly-Donabate service. *Neil Sprinks/MHCB*

Opposite page CLONTARF ROAD: Beyond Fairview the main line crosses the Dublin-Howth road at Clontarf. This view is from a Connolly-bound CIE train passing the Belfast-bound NIR 'Enterprise', with driving trailer leading, in August 1976. Liberty Hall dominates the city skyline with the Dublin Mountains in the distance.

A suburban station, Clontarf Road, now occupies this site. To quote the June 2000 edition of the Journal of the Irish Railway Record Society, 'The new station at Clontarf Road has built up a significant patronage from the nearby East Point Business Park, particularly from the south side of the city. Some companies provide a shuttle bus service for their employees.' In this picture, taken on 29 December 2004, work is in hand extending the platforms to enable longer DART trains to call, a reflection of the ever-increasing popularity of Dublin suburban rail services. *Both MHCB*

KILBARRACK: Preserved 'J15' 0-6-0 No 186 has charge of the 'Royal Meath' rail tour at Kilbarrack, in the north Dublin suburbs, on 23 May 1970. In the distance can be seen Howth Junction signal box.

This aerial view was taken four years later, looking towards Dublin, from one of the high-rise block of flats characteristic of this vast Dublin Corporation development. Not then complete, this part of Dublin became famous, or rather notorious, two decades later when Booker Prize-winning author Roddy Doyle wrote of it under the thinly disguised title of Barrytown. *A. Donaldson/Author's collection*

HOWTH JUNCTION: This view of Howth Junction on Christmas Eve 1979 is looking south towards Kilbarrack. The 11.10 Dublin (Pearse)-Balbriggan push-pull train is entering the station with the block of flats from which the previous picture was taken in the background. The palm tree adds a touch of exoticism to an otherwise very unexotic setting.

In the 'present' view, taken from the other end of the bridge, one of the pioneer GM Bo-Bos, 121 Class No 124, arrives at Howth Junction with a Pearse-Drogheda push-pull train in August 1994. *Both MHCB*

HOWTH JUNCTION: Preserved 0-6-0 No 186 curves on to the main line from the Howth branch with an RPSI special on 7 October 1972.

Twenty-two years later, in August 1994, a DART is seen at the same location. Palm trees, semaphores and signal box are all gone, although the GNR brick-built former station house remains. *Ron Elsdon/MHCB*

HOWTH: The 1612 to Connolly, behind Bo-Bo No 214, is about to depart from Howth on 15 July 1978. At the same location in August 1996 a Bray-bound DART is about to depart. Howth itself, one of Ireland's premier fishing ports, has changed considerably in the intervening 18 years. Although fishing is still very important, tourism has assumed great prominence, with a marina one of the town's newest features. *William S. Watson/MHCB*

HOWTH: What would have been a wonderful tourist attraction if it could only have lasted a little longer was the GNR tram line that started beside Howth station and climbed to the summit of Howth Head before coming down the other side to meet the railway at Sutton, the intermediate station on the branch. Car No 2 is seen beside Howth station forming the 16.27 service to Sutton on 21 March 1954. *Neil Sprinks*

Right and below Trams Nos 3, 4 and 7 stand at Howth Summit on 9 June 1956. The trams were withdrawn on 31 May 1959, and in August 1996 a 1990-built Alexander-bodied Leyland Atlantean of Dublin Bus stands at the summit on replacement service 31 to Dublin city. The trams had their own reserved tracks for much of their route, so the bus is not standing in quite the same place. It is close, however, for the white timber building on the extreme left of the 1956 picture can just be seen in the 1996 picture between the bus and the wall. *Neil Sprinks/MHCB*

Right HOWTH: Tram No 6 comes rolling down from the summit on 23 June 1956. No fewer than four Hill of Howth trams have been preserved, at Crich, Derbyshire; Cultra, near Belfast; the Orange Trolley Museum, California; and at the Irish National Transport Museum at Howth itself. *Neil Sprinks*

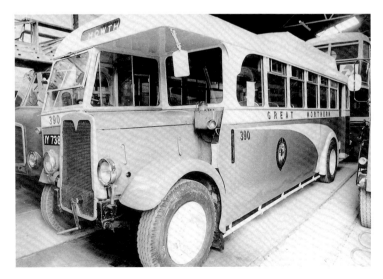

Middle and bottom A GNR AEC Regent bus, bound for Dublin, waits at Howth. Note in the foreground the railway lines that used to lead to the docks.

Howth is now the home of the Irish National Transport Museum, which owes its existence to that indefatigable preservationist Michael Corcoran. On display there in August 1996 was GNR-designed Gardner-engined single-deck bus No 390. Behind it is a GNR AEC Regent double-decker, virtually identical to the one in the previous picture. *Author's collection/MHCB*

MALAHIDE: Approaching the station on 28 May 1955, GNR 'VS' 4-4-0 No 206 *Liffey* has charge of a Dublin Amiens Street-Belfast Great Victoria Street express. *Neil Sprinks*

Middle and bottom GNR 'T2' 4-4-2T No 66 enters Malahide station with a stopping train from Dublin Amiens Street in about 1938.

The DART system has now reached Malahide. The low winter sun highlights the complex overhead wiring above a 2900 Class DMU departing for Dublin Connolly, and the 8510 series DART EMUs in the siding on 29 December 2004. *Henry Casserley/ MHCB*

MALAHIDE is one of the best-known stations on the Irish Rail system, for it is the finest surviving example of classic GNR architecture with ornate ironwork, handsome awning and attractively coloured brick and tilework. Designed by W. H. Mills in the 1890s, it frequently wins awards for its beautifully cared for gardens, foliage and flowering plants. In this picture, dating from 1979, the paintwork is a not very inspiring grey, a colour to which CIE and a good deal of the rest of the Republic was much addicted at that time.

By the end of the decade Ireland had become much more colourful and a cheerful, rich deep blue had replaced the grey at Malahide. The main entrance on the up side is seen here on 29 December 2004. The adjoining former station master's house was in the process of being refurbished and advertised as a highly desirable property in this highly desirable seaside area on the outskirts of the city.

In the third picture a Drogheda-Dublin Connolly four-car DMU with No 2953 leading approaches Malahide on the same day. The 2900 Class railcars are built by CAF in Spain, No 2953 being delivered to North Wall, Dublin, in the autumn of 2003 and working trials in November of that year before entering passenger service. Railcars are taking on more and more suburban and long-distance work on the Irish Rail network. A purpose-built Commuter Railcar Service Depot, costing 42 million Euros, was opened at Drogheda in the autumn of 2003. Employing a workforce of 55, each of IR's 144 railcars visits the service depot every second night. *All MHCB*

MALAHIDE: A long causeway carries the railway over an inlet from the sea immediately north of Malahide station. In August 1975 the Dublin-bound NIR 'Enterprise' is hauled by a 101 Class Bo-Bo as it crosses the causeway, while in March 1994 an Irish Rail Drogheda to Dublin (Pearse) push-pull unit is being propelled by a GM 121 Class Bo-Bo. *Both MHCB*

Above and right **SKERRIES:** Immediately south of Skerries in August 1971, the standard GNR-design signal box can be seen in the distance as the up and down NIR 'Enterprise' expresses behind 101 Class Bo-Bos pass each other. In the second picture a CIE GM Bo-Bo with a northbound stopping train pauses at the station in August 1980. *Both MHCB*

Right Resignalling as part of the upgrading of the international main line has rendered the signal boxes on this section, and the semaphore signals, redundant, but Skerries box was still there in August 1996, with a tall mast for CTC in front. *MHCB*

Broadstone to Maynooth

BROADSTONE, Dublin's MGWR terminus, was always the least busy of the city's main-line stations, and with the amalgamation of 1925 it became possible, by re-instating the link at Glasnevin Junction, to divert its few services to Amiens Street and Westland Row, rather nearer the city centre and, of course, convenient for connections to the north and the south-east. The last train was a cattle fair special, which departed on Sunday 17 January 1937. However, the locomotive depot survived for a good while longer, and in this early post-war picture a variety of engines can be seen, including, from left to right, No 673, a GSR-built 'I3' Class 0-6-2T, a 'J15' 0-6-0, No 606, a 'J19' 0-6-0 built at Broadstone in 1887, and another 'J15'.

Broadstone shed closed in 1961, but even this wasn't quite the end of the railway presence there, as the extensive buildings and yard had been taken over by the Great Southern (later CIE) provincial road services. In the 1969 picture the last section of track serving Broadstone, along which the occasional oil and stores train still ran, has been almost engulfed by grass and weeds, while derelict Leyland Tiger PS1 and PS2 buses await demolition.

Twenty-seven years later withdrawn Dublin City Bombardier double-deckers stand in the same spot. In the left distance can be seen the rear of the terminus buildings.
Adrian Vaughan collection/MHCB (2)

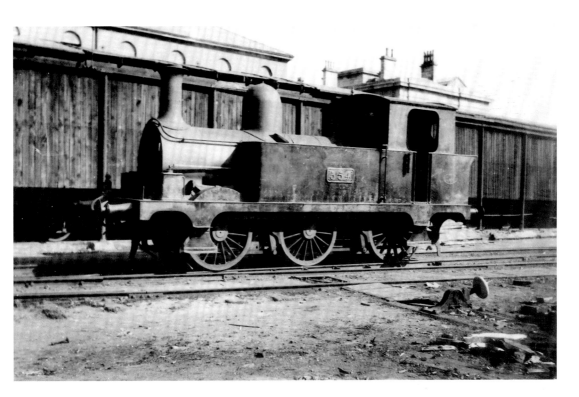

BROADSTONE: No 554, a Sharp Stewart 'J26' 0-6-0T built for the MGWR in 1891, stands at Broadstone on 17 September 1929. The roof and chimneys of the terminus building can be seen above the cab roof. The 'present' view shows the same location in December 2004, providing a clearer view of the terminus. *Henry Casserley/MHCB*

Right A reminder of the MGWR terminus in a nearby street, photographed in August 1996. *MHCB*

Above BROADSTONE: This is the single track from the terminus looking towards Liffey Junction, disused but still in place, in August 1969. *MHCB*

Below The telegraph poles remain beside the trackbed between Broadstone and Liffey Junction in 1996. Proposals exist to use the trackbed for an extension of the LUAS light rail network from Finglas by way of Liffey Junction and Broadstone to the city centre. *MHCB*

Right LIFFEY JUNCTION was where the line from Broadstone and the Liffey branch of the MGWR met. In this scene from the late 1960s the station was still more or less intact, although disused, and the sidings were used to store condemned stock, such as the covered van seen here, still bearing the original CIE 'flying snail' symbol, prior to its final journey to Mullingar for scrapping. *MHCB*

Below Liffey Junction in August 1996: the Loop Line curves away to the left, while the broken original line to Broadstone disappears into the weeds on the right past the old water tower. *MHCB*

BLANCHARDSTOWN: The Woolwich 'Moguls' were the principal motive power on the Midland main line from their introduction in 1925 until dieselisation. No 381 speeds through the disused Blanchardstown station, 4½ miles from Broadstone, with a Westland Row to Galway express in June 1954.

With the inauguration of the suburban service to Maynooth in 1981, a new station was opened nearby at Castleknock. In August 1996 an RPSI special, hauled by former DSER 2-6-0 No 461 and bound for Mullingar, approaches the new station. *Neil Sprinks/MHCB*

Above LUCAN NORTH: Beyond Clonsilla, 7 miles out, the Midland main line becomes single. One of the big ex-MGWR 'J5' 0-6-0s has charge of a Westland Row to Sligo train, composed of a very mixed bunch of carriages, near Lucan North, 9 miles from Broadstone, in June 1956. *Neil Sprinks*

Below For almost its entire length as far as Mullingar the railway runs parallel with the Royal Canal, bought by the MGWR in 1844. Here the August 1996 RPSI special is seen between Lucan and Maynooth. *MHCB*

MAYNOOTH: In December 1981 a push-pull set formed of former AEC/Park Royal railcars has just arrived from Dublin Connolly with a then recently inaugurated returning early morning suburban service. In the distance two 001 Co-Cos wait for the road with freight trains.

A completely new station has been opened at Maynooth to cope with ever-increasing patronage. A pair of 2600 railcars stand at the down platform having arrived on a commuter service from Dublin Pearse in December 2003. The spire of Maynooth Cathedral can be seen in the distance. *Both MHCB*

North Wall Yards

NORTH CITY MILLS: Retracing our steps back down the Midland main line and past Liffey Junction we come to the three-quarter-mile North City Mills branch, which served the Shandon Park Mills. This establishment dated from 1848, having been originally an iron foundry. It failed shortly afterwards, becoming known as Merton's Folly after its owner, but did much better as a flour mill. In 1969 a C Class Bo-Bo shunts wagons at the mill. Waterlogged barges that once delivered grain lie abandoned in the canal.

In August 1996 much of the building, out of sight in both pictures, has been converted to flats, the railway has gone, and the abutments of the bridge, demolished one Sunday in 1990, can be seen. Part of the complex is still a bakery. The canal has been cleared and some of the lock gates repaired, although a culvert blocks its re-connection with the Liffey in Dublin Docks. *Both MHCB*

Above GLASNEVIN: In 1975 a transfer freight from Islandbridge to North Wall hauled by 201 Class Bo-Bo No 218 rounds the curve by Glasnevin Cemetery and is about to pass over Glasnevin Junction; the line on the far left is the Liffey branch from the Midland Yard at North Wall to Liffey Junction. *MHCB*

Below left and this page GLASNEVIN: These four views of traffic at Glasnevin were taken from a footbridge, known locally as the Iron Bridge. In the first, from August 1972, 201 Class Bo-Bo No B212 heads a North Wall-bound freight past the site of Glasnevin station, closed in 1907.

The second photograph shows one of the heaviest passenger trains on CIE in the 1970s, the up daytime 'Cork Mail'. After calling at Heuston station it reversed back to Islandbridge Junction, then continued on to Dun Laoghaire to connect with the evening Holyhead mail boat. The 13-coach train is seen here hauled by Co-Co No A22R. The third vehicle is GSWR diner No 2092 dating from 1915 and not withdrawn until 1972.

Heavy freights were sometimes assisted up from North Wall past Glasnevin, as seen in the third view, dated August 1973. No E429, a 400hp CIE/Maybach diesel-hydraulic shunter built in 1961, banks a train of four-wheel container wagons. The North City Mills can be seen in the background directly above the shunter.

In August 1996 a freight train from North Wall hauled by a GM Bo-Bo heads towards Glasnevin Junction. The disappearance of the allotments and the growth of the bushes and trees in the adjoining gardens in the intervening 23 years will be noted. *All MHCB*

Above NORTH WALL: No 203, an 0-6-4T built at Inchicore in 1879, shunts at North Wall MGWR yard in the early 1930s. The bridge above carries the line from North Strand Junction to Amiens Street GSR station. *Author's collection*

Above right and right The same bridge is seen in the background of this March 1975 photograph of CIE Bo-Bo No 214 shunting the entrance to the MGWR yard at North Wall. In the distance, beyond the bridge and above the locomotive, is Connolly locomotive depot, while the steeply curved single track on the right connects the MGWR line at Newcomen Bridge Junction with the DSER side of Connolly station.

In the March 1994 view the line from Newcomen Bridge Junction to Connolly has been taken out of use temporarily, and the trackbed blocks the Royal Canal's access to the Liffey. A 121 Class Bo-Bo stands on the main line shunting a rake of carriages into Connolly station. *Both MHCB*

Below A panoramic view of North Wall in August 1996, looking north-westwards. In the distance on the extreme left of the picture can be seen the bridge in the previous photographs, with a train on it. *MHCB*

NORTH WALL: No B104, one of the CIE A1A-A1A BRCW diesel-electrics with Sulzer 950hp engines built in 1956, climbs past Church Road Junction at North Wall in July 1970, while at the same location in August 1975 are rebuilt A Class and rebuilt 201 Class locomotives. All the wagons in the sidings to the right are four-wheelers. *Both MHCB*

Opposite NORTH WALL: General Motors Bo-Bo No 166 is at work in the former LNWR yard at North Wall in August 1996, amongst the array of containers, mostly belonging to the now defunct Bell firm of Waterford.

There has been a worrying decline in freight traffic on Irish railways in the new millennium, it having disappeared altogether from Northern Ireland. This area, known as Spencer Dock, was being redeveloped in December 2004, although the rail presence will not disappear entirely as a new passenger station is to be built here to relieve the pressure on the commuter traffic at Connolly from the Dundalk and Maynooth lines. *Both MHCB*

This page POINT YARD: This former GSWR yard, with wooden-post semaphore signals prominent, was photographed in April 1980, but by August 1996 the signals had gone, only one track remained for access to the port, and the Point Depot was then Dublin's principal venue for pop concerts. *Both MHCB*

NORTH WALL: Four views of the former GSWR yard at North Wall. The first was taken in August 1970, and shows 1961-built CIE/Maybach shunter No E424 shunting.

Six years later, in August 1976, Nos E427 and E424 are still at work – note the plethora of four-wheeled wagons. In the centre background is Sheriff Street signal box, with the Point Depot and North Wall docks beyond.

In the third view, dated 10 August 1977, the last active 101 Class Birmingham/Sulzer A1A-A1A, No 106, enters the yard with an oil train from Inchicore.

Right until the final withdrawal of the class in the autumn of 1995, the 001s were a familiar sight at North Wall. Here No 036, with another last survivor in the distance, shunts in April 1995. *All MHCB*

95

Left ISLANDBRIDGE JUNCTION: Having just emerged from Phoenix Park Tunnel, 001 Class No 021 is about to cross the Liffey and approach Islandbridge Junction with a down freight in July 1985. *MHCB*

Right This closer view of the junction shows the Liffey bridge in the right foreground. A rake of Mark III carriages is shunted between the signal box and a GM Bo-Bo in August 1996. The track on the left is now platform 10, part of the Heuston station redevelopment. *MHCB*

Right and below ISLANDBRIDGE JUNCTION: Looking towards the junction from Heuston station, A1A-A1A No 107 with the Inchicore Works-Heuston staff train passes a CIE/Maybach shunter in August 1969. In August 1974 another A1A-A1A shunts the Guinness yard while GM Bo-Bo No B161 arrives with an up express. *Both MHCB*

Left HEUSTON YARD: Three views of goods stock contrasts in Heuston Yard. The first shows an inscription on a departmental wagon in August 1969. *MHCB*

Below A pair of GSWR-built horse-boxes, August 1970. *MHCB*

Bottom A GM Bo-Bo shunts container flat wagons with keg containers in December 1995. *MHCB*

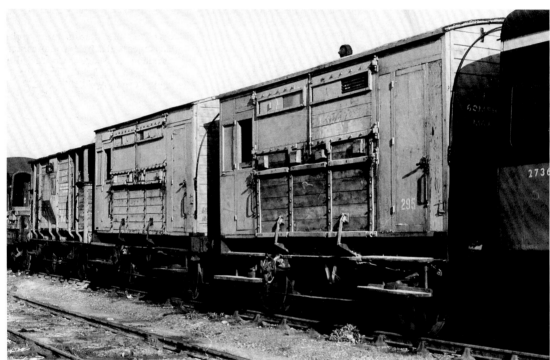

HEUSTON YARD: In the first of a pair of passenger stock contrasts, on the left is a former DSER six-wheel passenger brake in departmental stock, and on the right brand new CIE BR Mark II air-conditioned standard No 5218, in August 1973. *MHCB*

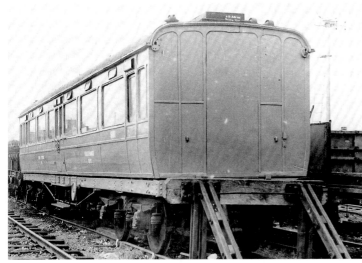

One of the handsome bogie carriages built by the Lancaster Carriage & Wagon Co for the MGWR in 1902 and in departmental use in April 1975. *MHCB*

HEUSTON is the location of the headquarters of the Irish Railway Record Society. Founded in 1946, it is impossible to overestimate the work of the Society in recording every aspect of the Irish railway scene, to say nothing of its careful preservation of a rich variety of documents, photographs and artefacts. *MHCB*

KINGSBRIDGE/HEUSTON: Ireland's most famous and powerful steam locomotive, No 800 *Maeve*, leaves Kingsbridge with a Cork and Killarney luncheon express in May 1946.

At the same location in December 1995, with the carriage servicing depot built in 1975 in the background, a 2601 Class railcar arrives at Heuston from Kildare. *J. Macartney Robbins/MHCB*

KINGSBRIDGE/HEUSTON: No B234 arrives in August 1969; this was one of two C Class Bo-Bos rebuilt with Maybach 950hp engines in 1966.

In the second view, taken on Friday 1 August 1980 (the day before the August Bank Holiday), No 058 arrives with the 1800 from Waterford. This train had been severely delayed on account of the worst accident in recent Irish railway history earlier that day when the 10.00 Heuston to Cork had been derailed at Buttevant with the loss of 18 lives. The leading vehicle is a Dutch-built heating van.

The 'Cu Na Mara', the 11.00 from Galway, approaches Heuston on 28 December 2004 hauled by GM 3,000hp No 218. The carriages are known as the International Set, BR Mark IIIas, built at Derby and intended as prototypes for an export fleet. *All MHCB*

KINGSBRIDGE/HEUSTON: GSWR '400' Class 4-6-0 No 403 arrives at Kingsbridge with a Cork express in 1923. Delivered from Armstrong Whitworth in October 1922, but not put into service because of the Civil War until June 1923, this must have been one of No 403's earliest outings. Rebuilt from its original, unsatisfactory, four-cylinder form in 1934, it was withdrawn by CIE in March 1957.

The second photograph shows the Heuston signal box, originally Kingsbridge, erected when electrically operated colour light signalling was introduced in 1939 and removed with the current rebuilding and extensive track re-organisation. *J. Macartney Robbins/MHCB*

KINGSBRIDGE/HEUSTON: The afternoon train from Inchicore Works has just arrived at No 1 arrival platform in August 1970. It consists of two former GSWR carriages, that in the picture being No 861, a magnificent Corridor Brake Tri-composite, built for the Rosslare-Cork boat trains in 1906. This was by then the last clerestory-roofed and the last 12-wheeled carriage in regular passenger service anywhere in the British Isles. It was withdrawn shortly afterwards and very nearly fell to the cutter's torch, which would have been a tragedy of major proportions. Fortunately it was rescued in the nick of time to become the RPSI's first preserved carriage.

On an August evening in 1996 a more modern rake of carriages is standing at platform 2, formerly the departure platform. Carriage No 4101 is a standard, one of a fleet of ex-BR Mark IIs bought by CIE in 1991/2 and dating from 1966-9; this example was originally BR 1st No M5428. *Both MHCB*

Below A quiet moment on the new concourse for platforms 5, 6, 7 and 8, December 2004. *MHCB*

Opposite page and below KINGSBRIDGE/HEUSTON: In 1964 (two years before its renaming as Heuston) the interior of Kingsbridge station was quite extensively refurbished, the platforms being tiled in black and white and the general appearance being greatly improved. This is platform 1, latterly No 2, looking towards the concourse, on 4 June 1964. The carriage nearest the camera is one of the 2405 Class of buffet cars built at Inchicore in 1953/4.

Like so many early stations in Britain and Ireland, Kingsbridge consisted of one departure platform plus a bay, and one arrival platform, with a number of carriage sidings in between. This arrangement persisted for well over 100 years, and it was not until 1972 that an island platform was installed in place of three of the four sidings. In the second photograph, dating from the summer of 1971, carriages are being shunted on one of the sidings.

The final view, from April 1994, shows GM 071 Class Co-Co No 086 having just arrived with the 1730 from Cork. Two Bombardier buses are alongside ready to convey passengers to Dun Laoghaire, the present-day substitute for boat trains. *Harold D. Bowtell/MHCB (2)*

Right A curious combination at Heuston on 28 December 2004. Northern Ireland Railways No 8208 *River Lagan*, in 'Enterprise' livery, has just arrived with a relief train from Cork consisting of four Cravens carriages dating from the 1960s and No 3179, a British Railways-built Mark 1 dating from the 1950s, rebuilt to provide steam heating for Irish Rail's oldest passenger stock. Little effort seems to be made to schedule the 'Enterprise'-liveried locomotives to the Dublin-Belfast route, which is rather a shame. *MHCB*

This page KINGSBRIDGE/HEUSTON: The exterior of the arrival side at Heuston in August 1971. The buses are all CIE Leyland OPD2 Titans dating from 1950. Although not visible, the further of the two inside the station is standing on a section of still extant tram track.

Trams returned to Heuston in the summer of 2004 with the opening of the LUAS route from Connolly station to Tallaght. This provides much the quickest route from Heuston to the city centre and to Dublin's other principal main-line station. A tram crosses the ornate bridge over the Liffey alongside Heuston station.

The third photograph shows the refurbished and much extended main concourse in December 2004. *All MHCB*

Opposite KINGSBRIDGE/HEUSTON: The 7.45pm Cork Night Mail leaves Kingsbridge behind 'D17' 4-4-0 No 98 and Maunsell 2-6-0 No 382, newly repainted in green livery, in about 1947.

The second view is of re-engined Metro-Vickers Co-Co No A20R pulling out of Heuston with a Cork express in August 1969. No E405, a 1955-built 400hp shunter, is shunting carriages on the left.

The third picture is of the new platform 6. The signal at the far end of the platform is approximately where the carriage is at the extreme left of the previous picture. *R. N. Clements/ MHCB (2)*

INCHICORE WORKS (of which more will be seen in the next chapter) is 1¾ miles out from Heuston, at the summit of a stiff climb varying from 1 in 117 to 1 in 84. Aspinall 'D14' Class 4-4-0 No 60 of 1891 passes the castellated grandeur of the signalman's lookout in about 1948. Remarkably little, at least until the publication of Greg Ryan's *The Works* to mark the 150th anniversary in 1996, has been written about Inchicore, one of the oldest and most important railway works in Europe. Like Heuston station it owes its original design to Sancton Wood, and the first employees started work there in April 1846; the first week's wage bill amounted to £83 12s 9d.

The second, wider, view shows the east end of the running shed in August 1974, looking towards the castellated lookout and signal box. Beyond the two seated railwaymen is GM Bo-Bo No B166 and D302, one of the original CIE-built Mirlees-engined diesel shunters of 1947.

Looking in the opposite direction on 21 December 2004, the castellated tower is now the office of Greg Ryan, Iarnrod Eireann's Heritage Officer; in the distant running shed one of the last operational 121 GM Bo-Bos can be seen. Colour light signals control the revised track arrangement, including the one-time siding on the far right, which is now a third running line. *Real Photographs/MHCB (2)*

108

INCHICORE: No 500 passes Inchicore with a Limerick-Kingsbridge express on 20 September 1951. The first of three 5ft 8½in 4-6-0s dating from 1924, they were originally designed for mixed traffic work, but soon proved themselves ideal motive power for Dublin-Cork expresses.

In the second photograph pioneer Metro-Vick Co-Co No 001 passes Inchicore with an up express in July 1975.

Finally GM 201 Class Co-Co No 220 is seen at the same spot with the first up express of the day, the 0520 from Cork, in August 1996.
E. M. Patterson/ MHCB (2)

INCHICORE: In the first of these four views former GSWR 'D14' 4-4-0 No 60 pilots '400' Class 4-6-0 No 409 on a down train passing Inchicore in 1946.

In the second photograph, taken in July the following year, '500' Class No 501, converted to oil burning, passes with the 3.00 pm Kingsbridge to Cork and Killarney train. The photographs were taken beside the west end of the works, and it can be seen that the Dublin suburbs had been left behind and open countryside reached.

On 25 April 1955, the date of the third view, new housing forms the backdrop for 'D14' No 95 shunting at Inchicore. This is hardly appropriate work for a 70-year-old former express engine, and it was withdrawn a few weeks later and broken up at its birthplace.

The 'present' photograph shows a 2600 Class railcar passing the same location in August 1996 with a Kildare-Heuston service. *J. Macartney Robbins (2)/Henry Casserley/MHCB*

INCHICORE: '400' Class No 403 climbs away from Inchicore towards Clondalkin and the South West with the 10.30am Kingsbridge to Cork express on 21 March 1954.
    A few hundred yards further west, the 'present' equivalent shows a 2600 Class railcar forming the 0800 Heuston to Kildare service in August 1996. *Neil Sprinks/MHCB*

CHERRY ORCHARD: On 3 August 1977 GM Co-Co No 079 runs through what was then still rural County Dublin with the 1135 Cork to Heuston train.

In the spring of 1994 a new station, Cherry Orchard, was opened between Inchicore and Clondalkin to serve the ever-growing Dublin suburbs, and coinciding with the inauguration of the regular Heuston-Kildare railcar service. With five intermediate stops the 30-mile journey takes 50 minutes, and 15 down trains operate each Monday to Friday. In August 1996 201 Class No 210 *Abhainn na hEirne/River Erne* pauses at Cherry Orchard with what the working timetable described as the 0705 suburban passenger from Portlaoise. Although not scheduled in this timetable to stop at Cherry Orchard, in certainly did on this occasion and picked up a couple of passengers before heading down the bank to Heuston. The carriages are former early BR Mark IIs. *Both MHCB*

CHERRY ORCHARD: The three 'past' views from June 1956 show trains having just passed the site of the modern Cherry Orchard station, then still four decades into the future. In the first, immaculate, brand new, silver-liveried Birmingham/Sulzer A1A-A1A No B101 takes the curve between Clondalkin and Inchicore with an up express.

Many main-line services in the 1950s were operated by the Park Royal railcars following their introduction in 1951, and the second picture shows a three-car set, with a six-wheel van in tow, at the same location.

Finally, brand new Metropolitan Vickers, Crossley-engined 1,200hp Co-Co No A45 hauls an up express.

By the mid-1990s the Dublin suburbs had spread further west and a high fence made it impossible to exactly repeat the previous pictures. The view below is from the same bridge but looking eastwards towards Inchicore as a 201 Class Co-Co passes with an up express in August 1996. *Neil Sprinks (3)/MHCB*

Inchicore Works

The last section of our book concentrates on Inchicore itself. Always far and away the most important works and running shed on the Great Southern & Western Railway, it continued to be so in GSR and CIE days. Its chief rivals were the Great Northern's Dundalk Works and those of the Northern Counties Committee in Belfast. The former has vanished, the latter continues as a maintenance depot, but Inchicore, even if it no longer builds locomotives and carriages from scratch, is still pre-eminent. We begin with carriages.

Top In the first picture two suburban Brake 3rds are undergoing overhaul in 1969. Numbered in the 1893-9 series, their Inchicore bodies, dating from the mid-1920s, were mounted on underframes bought a little earlier from Belgium by the MGWR. That nearest the camera, No 1893, survived until the autumn of 1973 and was the very last non-corridor carriage at work in Ireland. *MHCB*

Middle On 16 April 1948 a four-wheeler of great antiquity has been reduced to little more than its chassis, and next to it, looking unkempt and abandoned, is No 36, the GSWR Bury single of 1847. It suffered a happier fate than the carriage, being restored and put on display at Glanmire Road (now Kent) station in Cork, where it can presently be seen. *Henry Casserley*

Bottom Fortunately another similar four-wheel carriage escaped oblivion, although only just, and is now on display at the Transport Museum at Cultra. This is No 48, an open sided, windowless four-wheel 3rd built for the Dublin & Kingstown Railway in 1844. *MHCB*

Another distinguished carriage that was very nearly lost to us is State Saloon No 351. Built as a Royal clerestory-roofed carriage by the GSWR in 1902, it was rebuilt with an elliptical roof in the 1920s, and used by the GSR and CIE on state occasions until the 1970s. It is seen here at Inchicore in 1970. Replaced shortly afterwards, it was stored out of use at Inchicore, neglected and very nearly destroyed in a fire.

A number of enthusiasts had been campaigning for No 351's unique value to be recognised and in 1995 a meeting was held between FAS (the Training and Employment Authority) and the Railway Preservation Society of Ireland. A programme for restoration was drawn up, much of the driving force for this being Charles R. M. Meredith, a well-known Dublin solicitor, jazz musician and all-round good egg! I doubt if a railway project ever received such exalted encouragement, for Michael P. McDonnell, the Group Chief Executive of CIE, Lord O'Neill, President of the Railway Preservation Society of Ireland, and Dr Garrett FitzGerald, the former Taoiseach, all lent their support, which culminated in the unveiling of the magnificent No 351 by the President of Ireland no less, Mary McAleese.

The third view shows Mr Meredith and the author's wife Maeve (named, of course, after Ireland's most famous steam engine!) in the Royal Saloon on 21 December 2004. *MHCB/Maeve Baker*

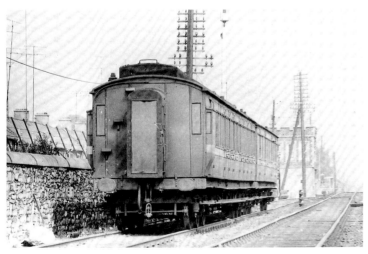

The Inchicore Works train waits to make its afternoon run to Heuston in August 1969. The carriage nearest the camera is No 861, a magnificent example of the coachmaker's art of the Edwardian era and now preserved by the RPSI. *MHCB*

Left From carriages to locomotives, and '400' Class 4-6-0 No 402 is seen standing outside the running shed at Inchicore in July 1956, being prepared to work a special to Cork. *G. H. Burton*

Below left No 338, a Coey 'D4' Class 5ft 8½in 4-4-0 built at Inchicore in 1907, was photographed at the same location in the 1930s. *Author's collection*

Above A line-up of locomotives outside the shed on 24 April 1955, with 'J15' Class No 200 and Maunsell 2-6-0 No 377 in the foreground. *R. M. Casserley*

Below The model of Inchicore running shed in the Transport Museum, Cultra, with a former Waterford, Limerick & Western 4-4-0, a former MGWR Atock 2-4-0 and an Aspinall 'D17'. *MHCB*

Three general views of the west end of the shed. The first dates from the 1930s, with a 'D4', a Woolwich 2-6-0, and a 'D19' 4-4-0 in evidence.

In August 1971 the scene is of a vanished generation of diesels; from left to right, they are Birmingham/Sulzer No B104, rebuilt B201 Class No B221, Birmingham/Sulzer No B101, rebuilt A Class No A25R, and shunter No E402.

Outside the shed in August 1994 are, again from left to right, a GM Bo-Bo, two 001s and a couple of generator vans. *Author's collection/ MHCB (2)*

The last C Class in original condition, No C220, is in the process of receiving its new General Motors power unit inside the erecting shop in August 1972.

Inside the running shed in August 1996, one of the last still operational original single-cab General Motors Bo-Bos, No 123, stands alongside GM 200 Class Co-Co No 210 *Abhainn na hEirne/River Erne*. *Both MHCB*

Left The scrap road at Inchicore in May 1950, with former Waterford, Limerick & Western 0-6-0 No 222 in the foreground. *Henry Casserley*

Below left No G601, one of the little 130hp four-wheel Deutz diesels of 1955, in derelict condition in August 1978. These were among the most under-employed of CIE diesels. I did once manage to travel behind one on the Loghrea branch just before it closed in 1975, and several, including No G601, have been preserved in working order. *MHCB*

This page No B113, one of the pair of original CIE-built, Sulzer-engined main-line Bo-Bos of 1951, is seen in the first view outside Inchicore running shed in August 1973. In the distance are the two GSWR-built corridor coaches used on the Inchicore Works train.

After withdrawal, No B113 lay at Inchicore in an increasingly derelict state for many years, and was photographed again in a sad state of repair in August 1993.

However, it was cosmetically restored to its original condition for the Inchicore 150 celebrations in the summer of 1996, as seen in the third photograph. *All MHCB*

Opposite page Ireland's most powerful steam locomotive, the magnificent Great Southern 4-6-0 No 800 *Maeve* of 1939, is seen here at Inchicore in early 1964 before being towed into preservation in Belfast. The second photograph shows *Maeve* at the Transport Museum, Cultra, in August 1996. *CIE/MHCB*

This page In the upper photograph 'J15' Class 0-6-0 No 186, with Belpaire boiler and large tender, and one of the not very successful 'J15Bs', the Great Southern successors of the 'J15s', pose at Inchicore shed in about 1955.

No 186 was one of two 'J15s' to be preserved; the other, No 184, is seen here in the second view stored at Inchicore in 1969. Behind is the DSER 2-6-0 No 461.

The third view shows No 186 at Inchicore during the 150th anniversary celebrations in the summer of 1996. To the left are vehicles for the new Dublin-Belfast 'Enterprise' services, while preserved diesel shunter No E428 can be seen in the distance. *Adrian Vaughan collection/MHCB (2)*

Above 'Dignity and Impudence' used to be a favourite caption for pictures of contrasting rolling-stock in railway publications of bygone days, and it is surely appropriate for this picture, taken during the Inchicore celebrations, of the diminutive but superbly restored GSWR 0-6-0T No 90 of 1875 – once part of a rail motor, and which can normally be seen at Tuam, sometimes in steam – and No 9101, a new 1st Class De Dietrich carriage for the Dublin-Belfast service. *MHCB*

Below The celebrations culminated in a well-organised Open Weekend on 16/17 June 1996, attended by very large crowds. Among the other preserved locomotives on display were No A39, restored to its original 1955 silver livery, and No C231 in its original green. Very fine they looked too, although neither, of course, was in original condition, both having been re-engined. *MHCB*

Finally, two views of one of the Driving Trailer Van/1sts for the new Dublin-Belfast service. Painted in a somewhat restrained livery of light grey, bronze and very dark green, this is one of 28 superb carriages that arrived from the French firm of De Dietrich during the summer of 1996. Each one is 23 metres long, fully air-conditioned, a striking, state-of-the-art, high-tech example of modern trends in main-line European carriages, more comfortable than anything to be found on the roads or in the air. One can only hope that the political situation will enable the £100 million investment in the upgrading of the international main line to be fully realised. *Both MHCB*

Index